LESLIE SIMON

COLLISIONS AND TRANSFORMATIONS

NEW AND SELECTED POEMS 1975-1991

COFFEE HOUSE PRESS :: MINNEAPOLIS :: 1992

Some of these poems have appeared in *Practising Angels, City Lights Review, The Berkeley Poetry Review, Heresies, Erotic by Nature, Left Curve, Oro Madre, Haight Ashbury Literary Journal, Synapse,* and *Xylophone.* The title poem "Collisions and Transformations" was inspired by a residency at the Djerassi Foundation in Woodside, California. *JAZZ/ is for white girls, too* was published by Poetry for the People/Free Spirit Press (San Francisco/Oakland) in 1977. Artaud's Elbow (Berkeley) published *i rise/ you riz/ we born* in 1981. Other work by Leslie Simon: *High Desire* (Wingbow Press, 1983).

Thanks go to Jerome Foundation; Minnesota State Arts Board; the National Endowment for the Arts, a federal agency; and Northwest Area Foundation for support of this project.

Coffee House Press books are available to bookstores through our primary distributor, Consortium Book Sales & Distribution, 287 East Sixth Street, Suite 365, Saint Paul, Minnesota 55101. Our books are also available through all major library distributors and jobbers, and through most small press distributors, including Bookpeople, Bookslinger, Inland, Pacific Pipeline, and Small Press Distribution. For personal orders, catalogs, or other information, write to:
COFFEE HOUSE PRESS
27 North Fourth Street, Suite 400, Minneapolis MN 55401

Library of Congress Cataloguing-in-Publication Data

Simon, Leslie, 1947-
    Collisions and Transformations : new and selected poems, 1975-1991 / Leslie Simon
        P. CM.
        ISBN 0-918273-93-5 : $9.95
        I. Title.
    PS3569.I4826C6 1992
    811'.54 – dc20   91-39498
                                                                            CIP

9 8 7 6 5 4 3 2 1

Contents

HEART PRESSED TO SKY

FEET ON THE GROUND

for Ellen Sugarman and Linda Ware

Collisions And Transformations

I am the chicken in the egg giving birth
what the wing is to the angel
what the breast is to the heart
I sing
I do windows
I do weekends
night flights
on the right nights
hire me
I am a poem

JAZZ/ IS FOR
WHITE GIRLS, TOO

Summertime Is Ripe

for Donny

When someone gives you flowers
you must put them in a vase
that is the ritual, it is the grace,
the thanks, the   O BABY
flowers-for-me-in-the-springtime serenade:
the color of red getting pink getting orange
getting hot, getting ready
for barebacked summer
I need the season, I need the change
ready for xylophone stepping
all over the place
take me back
take me home
to how it gets in August
100 dEEE-grees-at-midnight weather reports
wet and slow catching colds
on humid nights, no smoking in the delivery room
sheets, shot with love
I catch the time/ out of
midnight yellow velvet;
I step off the platform
onto the street
3rd-degree bare-feet BURN.
I need to do something
I don't have to today
to let the sun beat me out
beat me clean beat me raw
today
like that's
sitting-on-your-front-porch-watch-your-life-go-by-or-fall-in -
love
MUSIC

like that's horn and bass/ Simple Facts

he plays the piano: he plays me
flowers are ritual
love is red getting pink getting orange
hot jumping symphonies
Summertime is ripe
pluck it off the tree.

Me and the TV Stars

When I was 8 years old, a girl on the block told me I looked like Rosemary Clooney and I was glaaaaad because I thought she was beautiful and sang real good. Hit Parade. And everyone else liked Geeeee-zelle McKenzie the best because she was more beautiful but I always liked the ones people felt a little sorry for. Could not STAND Annette Funicello—everybody talking about how sweet she was. I knew she wasn't.

So when the grown-ups had a talent show, me and 2 girlfriends signed up for a singing trio spot. The guys in the band laughed at our 8-year-old selves and said they didn't know how they could accompany us but when we started blowing
> "Come on-a my house
> My house come on-a"

they knew just what to do and did what I didn't know then was called improvising. They did fine—made me happy. We were good and I stood in the middle because it was my idea and I looked like Rosemary Clooney.

A few weeks ago I heard about her now being 47 years old and her coming back after being 200 pounds and hallucinating and my 8-year-old self shivered. "I don't want that to happen to me." And my 28-year-old self wondered at women losing themselves to drugs, to food, to alcohol, to madness over and over again. So hard for women to be healthy when they're good. Women aren't supposed to be smart or write books or get famous.

All those suicides.
All those lost lives.

And there was Rosemary Clooney staring out of a picture that said she said she lost 65 of the 80 pounds she gained. O/ but she was different, her hands folded and her legs crossed like we were supposed to do in kindergarten and her face smiling.

Was she happy now?

on top of men beating women

on top of men beating women
are the banks
on top of men beating women
is the church
on top of men beating women
is the economiiieee
        no way to get the bills paid
        no way to get the ends to meet
television ads are fuel
car ads
the pretty blond limousine
the Marlboro man
the image, the masculine
        percentage point.
on top of men beating women
are   two jobs
        no jobs
        bad jobs
        boring destructive deceitful jobs
        9 to 5/6 to 12
        graveyard shift
        poison jobs
                the venom is your own blood
                the venom is your own blood.

on top of men beating women
are   3-car garages
        all-electric kitchens
        color TV's
        no way to get the bills paid
        no way to get the ends to meet
                Mr. Jones beats his wife.
on top of men beating women
are   6 people to a room

rats on the floor
your baby's eating lead
no way to get the bills paid
no way to get the ends to meet
Bernie beats his wife
Tony beats his wife
Al beats his wife
the connection is simple
the connection is All
it is great
it is terrifying

on top of men beating women
is Hollywood
Las Vegas
casino town
movie star city
you lost it
you lose it
you never had it
is the government
is the program
the master plan
to keep us down
women under men
men under all
with liberty and justice
with liberty and justice
the blood comes dripping down
the black eye the cut lip
"they never press charges"
"they always go back for more"
on top of men
on top of men
beating women
is
the mainline

the fuel pump

        go   to the root

        go   to the root

the source

the only salvation there is

Cut it deep.

Cut it down.

Gambler's Deal

the zeroing in
of these minds
on nothing
the circling
they do
without center,
like the emptiness
of a two-ton truck
pulling
the summer heat
cross-country
doubling its price
at each stateline
arriving
at county fairs
can't afford
to unload;
zero back
pick up more steam:
as heat sweats
it turns to clay
builds tombs
to the double
of nothing.
at Nevada
the odds are
tempting
they get off,
make a fortune
in the delivery business
on the isle of sorrow
the gamble of
zero times
everything

I mean,
Double it
You can't lose
Keep the truck
You can't lose
the zeroing in
on fortune
life lost
like in an ad
on the side
of the truck
grinning, fading
pretense
being very
expensive
the gambler's life
is very
expensive;
the Nevada widow
steps aside
as her man
divvies up
the double
of nothing.

The Judges

devils in the night
ride red transparent papers
devils in the night
sift through opaque mirrors
keep count of all the wrongs
the sins the petty thefts
and treasons;
pass judgments
greased with money and
expensive meals
greased with
      this is the way we run the state
      keeping quiet the troublemakers
      this is the way we rule the state
      laying dead the people wakers.

devils in the night
cast spells called execution
lynchings
the magic words they use
      ana ana anarchist
      commu commu communist
like potions
they rub these words, the devil's brew
the magic spells of hate and fear.

beware you devils
beware the air
come riding on the air
old ghosts
old ghosts come back
to haunt the devils;
come old ghosts
the Rosenbergs

come old Sacco and
Vanzetti
come in the night
to haunt the devils.

now the truth
we want the truth
your hangings
were a farce
old ghosts breathe truth
into the present
George Jackson's truth
is now the present
new ghosts breathe truth
into the present.

devil judges
still stomping
stomp the same old ground
stomp out the truth
but beware
smoke still rises
turns back to fire
becomes the fire
come new ghosts
whose blood is boiling
the steam is rising
devils, beware
new ghosts
are on the march
stirring up
us survivors.

JAZZ/ is for white girls, too

Jazz/   born by black people
grown-up and raised
by descendants African, some Caribe
but none white
certainly not Jewish
            (Gershwin is SOME exception

                Summertime)
Who am I to question
A beat.   To answer.
Some claim reincarnation.
Some claim 1/16th blood vein black.
I claim I want to play jazz piano
I know I never will.
            the silver slip
            of a truck
            rushes through me:
            eye glint
            head slant
            street sure.
    the music   SINGS   to me
            wordless waves
            shoulder slides
            sift out beat
            from tone and time;
            chiseled sea
            lovers skin
            schemes and maps
            inside your mind;
                    silver inlay: ebony base.
I make certain poems
offering and thanks
I make certain sounds

organ echoes
flute flight
click clack;
Drum bassdrum
Drum bassdrum
on the track
on the track
Southside/ sidewalk cracks.
hard   hot   cement
the sounds the el makes
on the way downtown.
I saw those faces stare at me
"little white girl"
I stared at them.
my mother said:
      no questions
      no pointing
      no staring, at the strange skin.
later learned
what Strange Fruit meant
at 63rd Street Transfer
"You live on the Southside?
That's where all the colored live!"
Eyebrows raised like
you poor thing.

Bird River/ Root Strata/ Crying Song
Honey,
Let me tell you something
moon mirrors on the sky
sunflashes on the steel bar star
Jazz means something
      I need a line out
      Some connection
      Some cord
      Some tie
      knotting me up,

people.
I need a line out
receiver
transmitter
speaker,
people.
I need   a connection.
I move   in
something, thick with sweat
get jumpy get hot
beg/ to blow my way out
drum my way out
pluck my way out
like a piano   BLUE
from a fight, a roll on the floor
alone, like friends again
like a horn, Yellow Saxophone
yellow wool New Jersey man
Chicago—Detroit
No Stop Express
Straight to the sky
No Stop Express:
could you pick up one grown-up white girl, pleeeeeze
63rd Street Transfer
I need/   to make offering
I need/   to make thanks

Jazz/   is for white girls, too.

Note: A Rahsaan Roland Kirk concert at the Keystone Korner in San
Francisco in the mid-seventies inspired the title of this poem. "Root
Strata" in the last verse refers to the title of one of his albums, and "Cry-
ing Song" refers to the title of a Hubert Laws album.

Rainy Day Jazz
is Beautiful is Beautiful

I was drawing
lips
practicing my
penmanship
all OVER a page
heard a long low love song
you know
the I-hate-to-leave-you-but-I-gotta-go
kind
looking for another pair of lips
gonna ease your time
gonna ease your mind
with
BABY
this particular horn blowing
"By the time I get to Phoenix"
long low love song
is precisely   NOT
what I'm after
yet somewhere
in that threat
the break
the losemanship
the hardship, of keeping one
only one, the one and only
my heart breaks
and I say
horn man   BLOW
your love note
saying
you are leaving
one more time

saying
I love you
too much
for that
Remember you do
Remember you do
In the A-wake-ning
of heartbreak
I remember
I love you
one   more   time.

No-Name Poem

new I am
to this world and
if someone had told me
just told me   no
I would not have
come
but no one told me told me
I'd be me and me
alone
an I an I down the
street
alone
walking down the street
alone
seeing things my way
(keeping my way mine and
your way yours) this
I world eye-ing your world
another way alone that's
how we're all the same we're
all alone and
in that same way I thought
I mean
(if I knew your way was yours
and yours alone) I
might not have come
might not
would have stayed one
with the world
at one with the world
in union
with no me   no I
a union
a union

a wombian union
an o-o-o-mian
omian O-men
AMEN!
would not
have signed on
signed up would
not have come out
would not have
come
new I am I am new
still fresh still
thought I mean
still think we
were the same
are the same
are the same
are the same
alone and   ONE.

baby's coming, Baby's Coming

down on the ground
I get ready
for you
for how you'll
come out
night waters
on my thighs
seagulls are herald
starfish are jewels
and O/   the horns
make my belly jump
at the coming
of you
sweet little
original sinner
Number One
the blessed act
that made you grow.

out of what
are you made
molasses on my mind
the iron supplement
the make you strong
mineral
from the ground
from a mine
rich/
mineral;
I develop a taste for it
like hard liquor
I could live till ninety
make it a habit
for you;

iron crosses
the placenta
but so does love
it pushes   UP
against the fertile wall.

somewhere there
I took off with a flute
smokestack wanderer
cloud green hills
I flew, like a gone bird
Gone Bird
is the song we stumbled into sweat
about
trumpet, tram-PEET
your feet
down the
cloud green trail
belly BEAT
"we're gone, man"
inside myself

      to you,   is the lazy place

      I linger at

      O   the melody
      is heaven
      eternity is time,
      little baby.

I want to make
a cloth for you/ to
carry you in
to/ wrap around
the growing belly
make it like they do

leaves/ printed in the
sand
fossil shapes
but this situation
is not simple
there is landlord
on our back
electric guitar
lives below
too much noise
I want to be alone
to rock you
to wake you
to talk you
sirens on the street
derricks/ dump trucks
garbage in the wind
no money's coming in
knock against my ribs
kick and say
it's all right
stalled on cloth dreams;
robes and shadows
is enough.

but O when you come out
dump truck
dumps the world on you
you gonna make it
not gonna take it
be ALIVE and
move this world
some other way
                    and wake it.

I RISE/ YOU RIZ/
WE BORN

Counterpoint

it is often referred to as the itch. the urge. getting your full satisfaction out of life. out of honey. the sweet wet dripping down between legs. after Satisfied. after Sanctified. After the rain, no one complains. just lie there, letting blood-filled organs, tissues, brains redo their molecular needs. cellular renaissance. voodoo dust. like magic/ is born/ a miracle. two bodies gave birth and fed.

this is cock to cunt to cunt to cock counterpoint. this is a blessing. o come o come. to bed.

OHMS resistance/ OHMS
OHMS resistance/ OHMS

vol-TAGE/ vol-TAGE/ vol-TAGE

energy eLECtric
energy eLECtric

OHMS resistance/ OHMS
OHMS resistance/ OHMS

vol-TAGE/ vol-TAGE/ vol-TAGE

energy eLECtric
energy eLECtric

the sparkle of your spine on my brow
the heaven of your scent in my mouth
the pleasure of your breath at my teeth
the languor of your leg on my head
the presence of our love in my womb
has Burst upon my sheet
o come. o come.
to bed.

July Fourth Baptism

1

a deep. a cold. a hard. a rushing river. a day of death and chance. a drowning. a water. a murdering water. into this water slipped a body. into this body rushed the water. "o my god! he's drowning!" the water from which he sprang surrounds him. takes him back to the womb of its devotion. there is no ceremony. this is no chosen death. this is death chasing us.

the people ashore are mostly silent. disturbed. wondering. finally, joking. then silent again. absorbed. not speaking. not really dealing. with death.

on the way home. we kill/ a big dog. he runs into/ our car. there is/ a big thud. we know/ he is dead.

2

a thread of light
the needle pierced
bone sharp
evident
a skull
flesh less
stricken
dead
enveloped in spirit
in light
bleached
white bone
bare bone
structure laid plain
laid open
upon this bone
a skull
inside the skull

a space
a cavern
the wakened tongue
a memory
the teeth
"bite your tongue!"
you ghost
you are dead and gone
what is this thread
of light i hear
its pressure
on my brain?
bear the light
the bones are
sacrifice
bleached white bag
o bag of bones

3
i called back my breath
and told the weeping
to stay quietly inside
that place where it came from,
but my body rose up
punching the bruise
to the surface of my brain
"nobody loves me but my mother,
and sometimes she be jivin' too"
the Blues
what it gnaws   is
the elemental cause
of our sadness
the aloneness
no two steps in any one foot
no two feet in any one boot

it rained all night in my eyes,
but i see as clear as i can now

cry your heart empty, honey
fill it up again
you gotta wash out the inner organs
you gotta test out the faithful friends
you gotta see where you're dreamin'
you gotta see where you've come
you gotta face the believin'
that empty dark night
is just no fun

your death is not mine
except for the grief
that makes me bleed
you death is not mine
except for the love
that makes me see

one day i'll be there with you
like a star on someone's back
one day i'll shine the heavens
forget my bones cramped in this sack
i marry myself to the future
to the love in lightning's thrust
i marry myself to the morning
to the sun spread over us

your death is not mine
except for the grief
that makes me bleed
your death is not mine
except for the love
that makes me see

i rise/ you riz/ we born

Menses
Man sez:
when i apply for waitress work
to tell him when i'm on the rag
so he can plan his schedule
around what HE calls a drag;
my friend Ish applies for work
it all looks prosperous
until they discover baby
growing in her uterus.
when she cries "discrimination"
he advise
erasure of the fault,
the inside beauty;
that we are women
is no pain
is no shame
i proud
you proud
we proud

i wonder at the blood
the fear of it
the power it might bring
the rose it is
the rose it grows
the pleasure that we nourish

i rise/ you riz/ it's rosey
the future, the full bloom
eclipse the wish/ Ish
with thunder
the day's descent
the gray rained out

by light,
storm it up
electric wonder:
the Spanish Rose
my mother Rose
she cooks good
just like yours
universally so
we itch and grow
out of that curled-under
cozy rosey posture
fetal undercurrent, we
trombone it home

i rise
you riz
we born

The Truth Is a Simple Idea

lone assassin theories proliferate
conspiracy plots counterpoint
the truth crumbles
before my eyes
from lack of recognition
it is the spearhead
of a dead arrow
no one knows its name
no one knows its face

I leave my graveyard-shift job
the morning after the Dan White riots
ghosts lead me halfway to dawn
they whisper: "we'll tell all
ride our backs
over the dead of the night
we'll tell all"

do i risk my own back
for the secret
the ever-humming
fast-breeding channel
to the truth
so hot
so hot
you touch it
and you'd better know
how to hot-potato handle it
all the way home

the truth is a simple idea
it is the liar who is a genius
the criminal mind
convoluting layer over layer

of lie
the truth is a simple idea
watch for it at the split
of dawn
at the crack
of sleep
at the opening
of shadow
the truth is a simple idea,
but it's a hard thing
a very hard thing
to know alone

The Rising Up

I had just come to California
state of the stolen gold and the hills.
state of the Pacific.
was asked to go south to Ensenada.
state of the blue and shimmering sea.
so I got this "Gypsy Ballads of García Lorca" thing
because I was beginning to feel like a gypsy
between the sheets
and he had a very Spanish name.
little did I know then who he was.
        (1936.
                the Spanish Civil Guard.
                        the execution.)
green. the song he sang to me. the Baja.
the lower. the underneath. the rising up.
for better or worse. I married the gypsy.
my sheets got very rumpled.
the wind went through them in the night.
floating me out to sea. until the rock crashed.
my bones sank.
and I loved myself, finally. in the deep.
back home again. alone in L.A.
I put Lorca on the shelves. but in San Francisco
poet heroes sang about Lorca
and I remembered the name.
        "they kill the poets," Alejandro said.
then I met Pancho. I learned they kill the poets
or they kill their poetry or they kill both.
a double devastation. a singeing of the soul.
a burning of the books. but they can't ever
take it from you.

the yes of the people
the we of the people

Victor Jara/ Kim Chi Ha
Billie Holliday/ Lenny Bruce
García Lorca/ Roque Dalton
Otto René Castillo
and all my poet friends.

"the people, yes," he said
anon anon anon
and on
and on
and on
they dance
After the Rain, Coltrane
After the Rain.

Note: Quoted lines from poems by Alejandro Murguia and Carl Sand-
burg. "After the Rain" is the title of a John Coltrane composition.

STREET BLEATS

Introduction

Street Bleats were inspired by the names of San Francisco streets. As noted by the poems, some run beside each other, others intersect, one of them becomes another. The poems address relationships in space and time. Not meant to be imitation Gertrude Stein, they merely suggest elements of her style. The double play is that they intersect and run parallel with some of her influences that until recently have been suppressed: African-American, Yiddish, and lesbian cultures and codes.*

In these poems, except for Coleridge, Brontë, and Harlow who are Euro-footnotes – dying, sighing gods – and Isis, who is the presiding feminist presence, the characters with Steinian names – Bessie, Bernice, Nellie, Blanche, Grace, Howard, Bertha, Rosie Lee, Hattie, Carl, Irving, Rose, and Lily – might be black or Jewish, lesbian or gay. They might be your next-door neighbor or the people in the house down the street. They would never have met Gertrude's friends. She would not have invited them into her salon. But she sure knew they could talk.

In a few of these poems meaning is held off, sunk down, but not gone; the words are never entirely wrested from reference. In most of the poems meaning is close to the surface, more transparent, less opaque. It is that sinking and surfacing about words that interests me. Desperately clinging to narrative, these poems have survived the smashed syntax, the Steinian shipwreck. Trace elements are tribute to the chaos of wide waters below. Transparency is trance and works like a charm (or an alarm).

Leslie Simon
Fall 1990

*Note: See my essay "They Mine. Whose Mine? The 'African American Presence' in the Literature of Gertrude Stein"; Maria Damon's doctoral dissertation (Stanford University, 1988) *The Poetics of Marginality:"Minority Discourse" in American Modernist Poetry;* Judy Grahn's *Really Reading Gertrude Stein* (Freedom, CA: The Crossing Press, 1989).

Taking Bessie to Manchester

Redness. the air of every. it filled her heart. that red. she was struck. the speed (the deed, a reed) at which. the notion. reached her brain.

rock in hock. oh shock. the lock. the lock. oh cock. oh. oh. mock.

at which the red filled her heart. the Redness. that thing. simple spread. sandwich bread. red fill/ at will/ her heart/ that part. refrain, disdain. eat it. Now.

which rock? oh hock, not to mock.

and still it was, handily, handily. O Christ. you, too? we two.

I do. I do. I do. We three is me. don't you see? the cock the sock the lock.

Did Rock. Did Rock. Did Rock.

Taking Bessie to Manchester.

Bernice got next to Isis

something for her lips. oh dare, oh share. something for her lips.

a lick of chord to horde. a gentle slice of flesh be blessed.

the street's in heat, discreet. the street's in heat. bottles bunched, bouquet-like at her curbs.

a wonder, that thunder.

the very angle of her eye. what lie between her sigh. the very angle of her eye. oh my. oh thigh. oh, oh hi!

iron and dust. metal and lust. they sly. they sly.

Bernice got next to Isis.

Nellie gives into Blanche

Nellie named her Blanche for white and French. two things she never was. because. because she thought her girl would curl. her girl would curl another time. another time and place.

her face. was black.

her hair was thick. she never hid her looks. she took them where she went. and loved herself in health. she loved herself in health.

the beauty that she was. because. because she was herself. wherever that she went. she lent. her beauty where she went.

her mother gave her love a dove. she gave her love a dove. called it white and Blanche.

her daughter found another bird. she called it black and raven. she found her own. she found her own sky haven.

"mother, don't you see," she said. "I'm your girl, but I curl around another time and place. my face is mine and fine. my face is very fine."

her mother turned to look. she saw a sparkle. there. and so, a glow. "I know," she said, "your face is yours and fine. your face is very fine."

Nellie gives into Blanche.

Where Grace and Howard meet

buried a tree. its seed. when they were young. that dance, the chance. it took to grow. those roots, that foot. the tears, those years. the faith and joy, but coy. she was. in fact, she was too coy.

he wept. she leapt. from out his arms. he wept. she crept back in. his charms. outside, the tree spread seed.

outside, the tree spread seed.

it was with bounce she had her say. he heard her word. to pounce, to pounce was not the bell. "oh, hell, that's not the bell," she said.

and led him to her gate.

a leafy sound. a rustle, there's my mate.

please wait, it's not too late. please wait, this love's our fate. the bark to climb. the bell to chime. Now. there's the time. there's the sweet. the sweet, sweet time.

inside, the tree with glee spread seed.

the tree, with glee, spread seed.

Where Grace and Howard meet.

Bertha runs into Rosie Lee

in a webful weave. she saw her fate. too late. she saw her fate, too late. she saw the girl who lured her home. turn down the street, complete. with dude on arm. alarm, alarm. with man on arm.

"well, girl, you look so fine. in fact," she thought aloud, "you look sublime."

Rosie Lee showed off the man. her friend,

poor Bertha wept, but kept, it to herself. she left her dearest love alone. she left her love alone.

her heart was caught. her leg tripped up. the stumble stopped before the fall. she caught herself before she fell. and called to Rosie Lee,

"fare well."

she called out, "girl," and then she turned

her back on them. that man disarmed. her lover, charmed.

"girl," she said, "be well."

Bertha runs into Rosie Lee.

Coleridge runs with Brontë

those two. they formed a crew. and saved the rest, from dying. they soon ran down the hill and off the fence, suspense. a smell, so sweet. the street, like flying.

tickled and smoke. a feathered toke. the belly, crying.

"hungry, dear?" I fear, you're lying. in a quake. the road is quick, and blinding.

"do you see?" o say, I do.

now, find me, siren. sighing.

Coleridge runs with Brontë.

Harlow

alone, one bone. she called that home. rezoned, and gnawing. the air was cold and cold did catch. the actress, clawing.

alone, one groan. she died, and us, while striving for the stars, we spied. the gods to guide. though shattered their bones, and lying.

alone, no phone.

no one was home. so with a dumb and numbing moan, she left us, crying.

Harlow

Hattie went to Market

a biscuit, a basket. Hattie went to Market.

(Let Hattie be a prostitute, a call girl, or just an independent woman.)

a bliss it, a kiss it. Hattie said, "you can sniff it.

"just don't rip it, or rape it, or trap it, or take it.

"don't lock it or mock it. don't defame it or maim it."

such a sweet cake. a treat cake.

she baked it. she made it.

Hattie went to Market.

Carl becomes Irving

from that far and silent room there swept a broom. a bray of
light. a muffled sound. a groom.

but his lover left him, bereft. so now he was no one. he was no
one.

he crushed the broom into the mirror and brushed his face. like
love, it felt. it felt like love. he wondered how queer that is, how
queer.

and then he knew, how dear, that one. had become.

he gave him self, and self he was. and blooming.

the lover is the one who unclothes your ugly fear. disclosing
self to self. repose, he chose. and wisely.

for now he knew the lover is the one who gives you self. your
friends all say: "how well you look. how love becomes you."

it is only that one. has the other, become. and the other has
become the one.

so that you be *never* no one.

Carl becomes Irving.

Rose is beside Lily

who had the itch. stitch to stitch. they came down, laughing. a flower pinned to Lily's ear. stuck through her sister's nose, oh, that Rose.

which street to cross, which beau to toss. they cautioned each other, successfully.

when Rose married first, Lily cried. in fact, she almost died. then she found one, too. a husband, luckily.

for years and years they lived apart. until one day. Rose woke with a chill. her Lil. had died, unexpectedly.

Rose mourned, "I've lost that one and I can't go on."

that night she called her own girls to her side to say. "my girls, don't stare. don't look at men and forget the one. who scratched your nose, and pinned a flower to your hair."

then Rose went to cry at Lily's side, her sleeping twin. and there she died.

Rose is beside Lily.

Who's following who, Gertrude Stein?

wresting words from old reference
you refer us to sound
that is the jazz talk
the black talk
that thought thinking
you do
that sing sighing
that swarm swinging
that look liking
you blew

some called it
girl loving
some called it
Jew, that
mama loshen,
tongue without
country
the deterritorialized
blues

I heard
something else
that jazz walking
that black talking;
did you ever
credit that,
where that credit
was due?

HEART PRESSED
TO SKY

My Father, My Mother/ Myself

in his palm
cupped for warmth
burned a cigarette;
thirty years later
death was a relief
pressing on his tongue

with her umbrella
she crowds the night
against the rain;
focusing,
she is satisfied

yesterday was a cavern
I turned my head
into it,
a relief to awaken
one bone, one muscle
at a time:
unfolding
light

for my brother (after a heart attack)
at age 30

the heart is a bubble immune to cancer. it succumbs, however, to collapse. it is a tree whose sap is filled with metal. it twists from iron, a natural mineral, and turns, unnatural, in the air.

as a child she learned to breathe. tentative. afraid of the power life could bore a hole and bring up. afraid of vomit. the loss of belly. disappearing innocence. that we die. oh, that we do. afraid of killing and blame. that mild stroke over the head.

pleasure is the doing in of this dying.

pleasure is the absence of the eros.

the flowers only a brother could bring and weep, and, no shit, sweep into the air. gift, schmift. still, it is dear, life.

don't ya know? I love you like a brother, my only brother.

May 2, 1990

after twenty-five years
twenty-five years ago today
at the twenty-fifth anniversary
(so many ways to say)
my father died,
my brother and I talk
now, we've talked before
we talk at holidays
sometimes on weekends we talk
when our kids visit each other
we talk at weddings
we talk at coffee
we talk and don't talk
all (you know how that goes)
at the same time
we say:
I the sister older and almost grown
remember him so well
we say:
I the brother younger and not yet formed
blank him out
I the sister am angry
about all you have forgotten
I the brother am angry
about all you have remembered
Today brother says to sister:
"Remember how you screamed
Remember the light streaming
in the window
It was a day like today"
and I am struck with the shock
that shut sound and light out
little brother recorded
big sister blanked out
there is after all a reason
for us to talk

My Father's Hands

there was the touch
that, first
the simple laying
quietly resting
remarkably gesturing
quality
about his hands;
grace, too common
a way
to put it
strong, inaccurate
there was a music
to them
plainly
a carefulness
that now,
          crashing
into story
after story
of grown women
then girls,
betrayed
by *their* fathers' hands;
I can say
there was
a loving way
about them
that now,
I am grateful
for
more,
than I *ever*
then
knew how

How do you say *heat wave?*

it was the month
purple blossoms
punctured sky
and yellow light
pushed through earth
into caves
it was the month
easy streets
gave up to weeds
a dance of asphalt
and blaze
the month
of love
and sideswiped
death
hello, territory
hello, sealed kiss
pressed flower
outrageous hat
symptoms
of and of
again
prepositional
proposition
orchids
and wine
wide, embarrassing
sentiments
such catch
of breath
and death
again
such
of and of

again
prepositional
proposition
and
love again

Resolution

you poked a hole in my heart
and the squirting river
smoked and steamed its way
into the earth
becoming rock and bone,
a treacherous place for bare feet
and souls

you slivered a knife
in my coffin
cutting me half-ways;
half-wise, I mended the rip
and lived to dance
on my own grave

you took my hand,
placed it over my chest
so I could feel the blood
and finally,
red-fingered and screaming
I sucked away my memory of you

Maintenance Poem

now I know
what they meant
by the myth
of sisyphus
the fool
pushing his rock uphill
just so it could
roll down again
a leak in your tire
a hole in your radiator
just can't get ahead
trying to maintain
and you just had a fight
and you didn't mean it
filling up holes
with air and water
that only run out
like money
like love

trucks come out at night
when the wind dies down
and I look for you
in the bed
curled up
rolled into
the black blanket
someone sewed
from two fur coats

making love keeps you
up at night
lazy in the morning
the sunshine yellow's

gonna see you
eyed red
you eyed me
and I you
in the bed
curled up
I come home

just can't get ahead
trying to maintain
it's no joke

Found Objects/ Found Love (City Haiku)

sweet orange umbrella
pointing up towards a dry sky
wish it were you here

golden old coin chest
forced open on the close ground
I saw you pass by

Number Nine in black
fading in the rainy day
luck comes to young love

lost garage sale sign
purple with long pink feathers
you notice me now

stained glass spiral shell
high window on narrow street
that familiar hand

Transmutations

In this week
which opened and closed
with small institutional fires
no major damage
no injuries
In this week
where I read
books of tropisms
fires of mad women
poems of baptism
In this week
where I rode around
in my car
with a red sock
on the seat
wondering *what*
was the meaning of this?
a trace of children
in my life?
or the red,
a burning sign
an artifact
coincident, significant?
In this week
where two old friends
visited
who have the same name
the same look, the same effect
on my brain
In this week
which isn't over yet
there was someone smart
who said
"there are no meanings

only events
maybe pleasure,
who knows?"
In this week
where some
invest pleasure
with meaning
and others
simply invest
In this week
I fell back
in love with you
now, go explain that

Untitled

I'm in this rose-colored room
I don't know how I got here
they call
telling me
to come to work
they say
if I don't
things will start
to fall apart
very quickly
I notice palm trees
and how the coconuts
fall to the ground
when you shake them;
the way I figure it
if I leave this room,
I get fucked at work
if I stay,
I get fucked by you
I'm staying, I'm staying
everything, everything
falls to the ground

FEET ON
THE GROUND

Black Wings Buried Underground

Vietnam War Memorial: Washington D.C.: Summer 1985

black flashing streak
sleeping onyx creek
bed of gold

    do I need a passport
        to cross
            from one end of my heart
                to the other?

when they went marching home
we folded up against them;
now, we spread black wings
and weep

      is the water ever
      is the water always
      is the water never
      Blue
          again

any way you cut it
it's half as good as
whole

one man chiseled open the guts of dead buildings
another cross-sectioned war wounds
cold green light turning white
    and bright
unto death: Neon Breakthrough

      those pretty sounds of destruction
      the grinding crashing smashing sounds
      but when you are   done
      there is   none   left

they say the architect of the Taj Mahal was either killed or disabled so that no building could be quite like it, that monument to love. with split hearts we say: NOTHING QUITE LIKE THEM EVER AGAIN.

so we build a restoration ritual
to reach the other side
the passport shrivels in a heap
we take them in our arms
and wish them sleep

and war no more
and war no more

> he told me the first color to appear after black and white is always red. it slips through the gate and hangs softly like a gesture. it is spare and raw. quiet, like some possibility still young. a small dot and drop of red. a slender tie on a bright white shirt. a slim chance. fingernails painted red on a black and white dress. black lines in tight air, pulled by insects as they fly their invisible routes. a black web. a white shadow. a red smudge of blood.

a bird half-buried
underground
a large stone bird
a big black bird
a winged thing
a creature
feathered with names
a grand rock bird
a treetop bird
see the bird
its wings are spread
in flight

see the sight
a black wing bird
a measured bird
a naming bird
its power is the light
reflection is a living
thing
a simple bird
a pretend bird
a metaphor
a memorial
the Vietnam War
Memorial
a large dark thing
a beautiful dark thing
a bird
a bird
half-buried
underground

Dialogue

she said she was happy
couldn't complain
told me I should obey the rules
ignore the signs
of starvation

she said, personally,
her life was great
couldn't be better, that
I should enjoy my fruits, not
get so brought down with truth

she said I should just forget it
she said I oughta shut up

she said she wanted to be friends
once I cured myself
of my negative habits

I said it was no addiction
she said that was denial
I said look who's talking
she said looks like you again
I was silent
she was speechless
and the empty air
pointed

Lamentations

A Jew: to such a world in such a time

Israeli invasion of Lebanon, 1982

what poison breathed
what wind caught
what eye crossed
and crossed again
the double self
against the self
(brother cousin
Palestinian Jew
sister mother
child of that child)
geography twists
into history's soul
from tension's air rises
a red smoke

from California to Beirut
from New York to Tel Aviv
the American Jew
witnesses
a double conscience

a shivering memory:
the gates of the ghetto
opened and closed
no one walked out
no *one* was left

now sits and grins
upon the head
of that same lamb
deformed
a new ever-horrified

slaughter:
I stand
and still,
still
a Jew
make warning
      no more of it
      no more of it
in my name

Compassion

And God said to the Jews:

"Behold My Children,
       I gave you the Inquisition
       so that you might know compassion;

       I gave you pogroms
       so that you might know compassion;

       I gave you the Holocaust
       so that you might know compassion;

       I gave you threats and sneers
       burned synagogues, and well-hidden,
       unnerving, silent anti-Semitism

       so that you might know compassion;

       and, it seems, in my befuddled state,
       old and unbalanced as I've become, I
       gave you Israel

              so that you could know finally
              what the mind of the oppressor
              looks like from the inside out

              so that you might know compassion;

Oh, my children,
what will it take before you learn compassion?"

Dia de los Muertos

tied loosely
but definitely
with blue rope,
wedged in wood
I place
your memory
in the grove

it's not much
a quiet act
but the neighbors
let you stay
two white crosses
with the names of
two children in black

planting them in the grove
under heavy rainfall
I find a split log
to wedge one sign
and a blue rope
for the other

weeks later
they stand there
still certain

such little openings
we have on this earth
a small grove of trees
above a noisy freeway

people stop and notice
who knows what they think

in this country
that sends money
to other countries
to kill children

who wouldn't
stop and think

Imprinting

the after print
of a baby curled
in that blanket
rolled up tight
inlaid
like fine jewels
on my memory

the fossil print
of a fish
or a leaf
on a rock
age-solid
with hope

the chubby
handprint
of a child
on clay
the mother
touches
and holds

the earth
picks a day
presses it
to her cheek
and the curves
lie forever
in time

I followed that story
and that one
and the one that followed;

all the cheap imitations
the imaginings, the post-
holocaust fantasies
and I scorned their unrealities

"but, mommy," my eight-year-old
daughter said
"if they told what would
really happen, there wouldn't be
any story."
and then I wondered
"just who is following who?"

Occupied Territory

January 16, 1991

the blueness, that pleasure spot
the place from which the story starts
where love is felt
just beneath the ribs, their cage a holy dome
the solar center
the light through water
and dark through stone
the soft place, where your soul sits
and where we come undone
and where, if we love, love
and, if we hate, hate
and if we see the wonder, wonder
wonder at the blueness
the darkness, the coolness
underneath the bony ribs
an airy space
the pit where grief arrives
and pleasures rise
where she awoke and he awoke
and then remembered —
the place where the war comes
and sits
and shakes
and rides
the space beneath the bones
the free spot
the sweet and simple blue spot
is occupied

L.A. Benediction

a cluster of neon and palm
such green grace
and ease
such balmy living;
crosstown
a medic is poised
over someone's cracked
chest
massaging the heart
back to
poverty and jail:
armed robbery
in the city
of the angels

oh, blessed be they
who open borders
and see

A Fable

she played the lottery that day
the morning of the day
after the last day
of her vacation
she thought that maybe
on top of the files and piles
on her desk
waiting for her comeback
would be placed
that clue
to the way out
that glue
she had prayed for
ever since
she had found
her way in
to the grim
world of work

"It's not the work I mind
it's the way
they make
me
sweat
for it,"
she said.
"I mean
if I
could
put bolt to bolt
and call
it a day,
I'd say, 'okay.'
It's not

the work
I mind
it's the grind-
ing
me up/ into piece/
after piece
of time: blessed time
this life is mine/ is mine?"

two ten-minutes paid
one half-hour
unpaid
labor
day after day
savor
the moment
you untie
the claim
they have
on your brain
savor
the moment
you dock the clock
and the boss
gets a whiff
of a slick
side of bliss
the day
the secretaries
get *their* say
and full, full pay

she went home
and swept and wept
and thought and fought
with herself
and called

one friend
and then
another
and said,
"Girls, this
has got
to stop."

so her friends
hopped
on a bus
and rushed
with a fuss
to her place
and raced
with a taste
for a way
out

they planned
and they planned
two by two
five by five, six by six
inch by inch
together, we can

and this
was the start
of the part
of the girls'
and the women's
the start
of the part
of the current working
women's revolution

Testimony

for Harriette Davis

one side caught
like the wind
in the breast of a tree
one side caught
by the twig
of another branch

machines turn
and twist

what law survives?

inside the Chevy van
the air cooled
he was already dead
inside the house

drunk,
he had beaten her again
and again and again
terrified,
she turned on him
the gun he had taught
her to shoot

she sobbed
at the death
of her lover
she rejoiced
at this chance
to be free

in the courtroom
sat a woman judge

a woman lawyer
even the bailiff
was female;
we hushed
and rushed
between the trial
"it looks good
we may win."

and yet, one thought
gets caught
and caught again

I am witness
to how we hurt
and hurt
ourselves
how we came to this

the answers complicate:
misogyny, economy, self-defense
I know them all
and so hesitate
 to say
what I see
but, witness
that I am,
I must testify
to the violence
in our brain
exploding
again
and again

Bay's Ball

1
a sweet sailing game
a green blank
the hand of my son
solid
a piece of wood
crack ball
crack air
team for team
Birds and Bears
Giants, the ways
of the Oakland A's
play-offs, 1989

2
small viewing screen
woman's bookstore
she says:
"I know it's a male sport
but I'm addicted"
politically incorrect life,
how sweet it is

3
OK, OK
so my old hometown, Chicago
is playing my current hometown, San Francisco
and you think you've got troubles
decisions, decisions

4
I see color, I see diamonds
I have a fever
I am taken, forsaken
home dish, three fried bags

a recent convert
I tell you: blessed
is the game
that sets you free

5
everyone wants to know the score
suddenly
my son has all the answers
my daughter and I
who usually
do the talking
sheepishly shut down
we walk heads bent, hands cuffed
into sex stereotyped jail

6
I'm signing up
I see the beauty in the long ball
the silent nonviolent swing
the sport of America
young thighs, oh my

7
anticipation
California World Series
New York
eat your heart out
apple schmapple

8
get your seat
did you get your seat
at the park
in the bar
on the couch
oh potatoes

enjoy your comfort
while the so-called
lucky ones
Bart back and forth
Bay crossings
until the quake
cracked the Stick
and we all knew
no one would forget Bay's Ball
for as long as they remember
baseball

9
at the abortion rally
my daughter gives a pro-choice speech
"A's Fans for Choice" up the ante
of the quality of the crowd
my son delights;
and the string
tying the game
and the quake
to women's bodies
is tenuous
but I'll try

Mother Earth came to the field
and we all had to pause
watching the gap
between one side and the other

Responsibility

for Caya and Sage

time opens into circumstance
the place where you were born
which body you came into
male or female, dark or light
which body you came out of
always mother, woman, womb

there is a soul to every thing
human hand has laid on
from this gentle trust
a population grows

> the earth is rocking
> oh, my children
> land is sliding
> lakes are freezing
> ice is forming on the wings
> the earth is rocking
> oh, my children
> watch the shadows
> of your dreams

intention is a moving wonder
freedom is a constant thought
the struggle is no slogan
it is the action
of body tied to body
the movement of slender clouds
through barren structures

this is the time you were born into
the time of silent fascism
the time of the fall
and of the revolution

the earth is rocking
oh, my children
land is sliding
lakes are freezing
ice is forming on the wings
the earth is rocking
oh, my children
watch the shadows
of your dreams

what place you take
which side you stand on
do you stand
oh, will you rise
        which body you came into
        which body you came out of
oh, my children
watch the shadows
of your dreams

Rites of Action

for Ethel and Julius Rosenberg

moon, spread like water,
when I was five years old,
over the silent
impact of snow;
I stood waiting
for the shiny gray Dodge
and my father
to come home

that spring
when he returned
the "Happy Easter"
greeting
to a gas station
attendant,
I said,
"Daddy, why
didn't
you tell him
we're Jewish?"

twelve years later
in spring
my father
died

eventually
I see
the hidden device
the grease
that pokes the motor
into action
under the hood

I begin to learn
my father
didn't really lie
you don't tell people
you are Jewish
unless you have to

       my grandmother brings me
       chocolate Easter eggs,
       reminds me to watch
       the Passover seder on TV,
       reads her fortune
       in the astrology column
       daily
       she has all bases covered

       the White Sox
       shoot Comiskey Park
       into the sky

       the Rosenbergs
       are executed

       no one tells me,
       except the morning
       the papers come
       to say
       McCarthy is dead,
       my parents celebrate

thirty years later
McCarthy is resurrected
but now we drive battered cars
and tell our children
the secrets
they need to know:

ACTION
a ritual
of transport

Ethel and Julius
we celebrate

your history
is everywhere

COLLIDING,
WE TRANSFORM

Winter Song

if the heart of winter begs for a light,
    give it
if the child places her mouth to suck,
    bend
if the wind pushes breath to ear, frozen,
    slowly warm the flesh

lying sleepless,
in her bed,
she is
a wreck of dreams
the fear of it
(a broken stem)

I know that number
the she-horse of nights: worry
this living wonder
the more you love
the more you have to lose

    I am a paranoid person. I was raised on worry. Always,
    I imagine the worst. I pay tribute to the gods. And I am
    humble before luck, chance, coincidence, weather,
    chemical, cave, and fire.

you see, love
is what makes
the matter
it is
what matters

the risk
the thin space
of sky

chiseled steel
sharp, glittering
I'll take my chances
on it

the more of it
the more
there is
to lose

this wind
(wide wing)
and breast
of love

A Crack in Your Eye

I want all my clothes to get big on me
I want to disappear into them
overgrown overcoats
large fedoras
I want the dissolution of all solids
the disappearance of hard surfaces
the challenge of invisibility
an identity full of holes
so holy there will be none of me
left

I wish for bravery
the ability to peer softly
around corners
and make them into curves

something I could carry over
when I cross over
something roomy
so free of entanglement
I could get lost in it

I want to go
where everyone I love who dies
is the lightning flash
of a summer thunderstorm

I want to be a small point
in large matter
an electrical current
of love

•

hearts bite into clouds
they split like aching tongues
a circle stopped at zero
a zero stopped at time

which way
you gonna blow
or go
to the heart
of this large matter

holocaust?
oh, rot!

computer missed
its cue
you say?
oh, no!
so, so
down
we go

or leap
into
another zone
but not alone

religion drugs the masses
I hand you this poem

•

its place is space
in your brain
and time
a leap
into another zone

98

but not alone

religion drugs the masses
but not this poem

     a bird, a heart, a wing
     a bird, a heart, a wing
         a crack in the sky
         a crack in your eye
     a bird, a heart, a wing
         a crack in the sky
         a crack in your eye

Home I

"there is no there, there"
                                    Gertrude Stein

He lives in San Francisco.
He comes from New York.
He is looking for a pizza.
I told him to go to Chicago.

San Francisco is a cappuccino town.

every place has its bend

the way you want it to be summer
there
the way you want to make love
there
the way the horn blows like a wind
there

it is your home
where you learned
how to read
climb billboards
cross streets;
ice slick, with winter
you reach into time
pulling out music,
a joke

sheets, fresh from the line
grass mown
laying limp
the summer's offering
to a tidy lawn

Oakland, Gertrude
is there, there

I know
I tasted the barbecue
at a corner store

•

in a place
where lilacs grew
like weeds
I faltered
then held ground
firm, like a shadow
to its body

purple and drunk,
it takes the bait
surrenders at night
a tender, faithful lover

like a shadow
I rose beyond reality
 and closed to immortality
the eternal grasp
what does not die: this fact
alone we go —
elusive mate,
you are a lie

•

the place where you came from
the place where you went to
draw a line
and watch it curve

to be a place
you have to be
something

that someone
can get to

a place can cure
sickness
if you get there
in time

that place
was prairie
became staple
to a nation;
it is a place
to be from
it has already
been gone to;
in the language
of the beast:
it is ravaged

•

I knew a town once
where the place
crossed a river,
spent a lifetime
on a bridge
worshiped edge
and meeting
daily

it was the kind of place
that when you got there
you always said:
is this the place?

and always knew
it was

Home II

"You know you are lost because you do not know where you have been/
circling you meet yourself. You have to consider that home."
                                    Meridel Le Sueur

She said: "I couldn't leave this place
until I felt it was home."

She said: "What you are
you leave
and become again."

•

She was a bright, pearl-like thing
tight and polished,   lurch
and quick
she entered

"Hi, Mom, I'm home!"

the hand broken off at the wrist
the sentence in the middle
the life at the sweet

broken at the clip
bare nerve and ash
thick blue pulse

a fish
a bird
a rock
in heaven

a cell
a roach
a blast
on earth

a wish
a dream
some stock
in heaven

She traveled
hard, small roads
where time bulged
on its course
and music
offered itself up
as medicine

She wandered
from what she knew
was the place
to tear and rip
to where she saw
was the place
to mend and heal

it was the first and last place:
it was always the same place

it was like this
for many years
and it would be like this,
she finally knew,
forever

considering her self
home,
she knew she could leave
and begin again

Incest Survivor

To Sing

Streaming from her mouth was a tightly strung row of blue balls. Pop, pop. Each one birthed itself innocent. Separate and silent, her tongue rolled over the surface, judging the elasticity of each ball, its ability to thrive or even its potential to survive in air.

There were no ID numbers or dates or weights. Not even a name to tell the one from the holy other, but she wept at the appearance of each brightly colored ball poised on her lip, a perfect sound.

She watched the stirring of melody tear her tongue from its tip, and as air rushed to meet air, she resolved herself again to sing.

To Dance

In the triangle between one bone and the other, lay the atmosphere of trees. Thin pieces of twigs and green light. Spilling out like a burst of leaves let loose from shaking, her bones took hold of her flesh and wounded the air so that when it fell, a pattern of light shadow hit the ground and colors pitched themselves back up to the sky where the sun agreed she definitely knew how to dance.

To Paint

It was silly this blank space. Everything else had gone so well, but something was beginning to happen, and she eventually commissioned herself to see. At first, her vision was clipped. What she saw she betrayed. Instead of the blood and knives, she drew circles of love until the circles of love reached the edges of blood and she wept at how hard it had become to paint.

To Write

She saw the formation of breathing, and its death in the world as it swirled. The no-say, the no-dance, the no-vision that stuffed itself into the air suffocating one voice after the other. She witnessed in her hand the stick placed on a shrivel of wood, ink to tree, a dyed herb on grass. This was what she was to do. Despite the horror, she always knew she had to write.

The Castro, San Francisco

the place where the virus
first took hold
in this town
has survived
it puts shoulder to shoulder
and walks as it weeps
or tears a wild heart
or picks a thin bud
cornered, but quick,
it resists
like a sharp poem to a threat
like a strong root to cement
like a wall or a road
or a show
or an ode
it goes on

Collisions and Transformations

Woodside, California

sitting in a boat-shaped room next to a spider weaving a nest of bark and fiber. above sound, breathing in space. histories given and taken. dialects spoken. witness to religious ceremonies of the heart. symbols of the intellect. manipulated materials. little stories. a bone on the path. a bone under my bed. rumors of snakes and false tricks. in the morning, bird sounds from a sacred box.

two cars parked and facing each other. newer tan Volkswagen near the glass doors and wall of the barn. older black and silver Riley near the open wood fence. over the fence, hills and fog. inside the glass, woven words and the madrone wood nest. the cars are poised, but they have nowhere to go for now. the elder makes a nice chaise lounge in the sun. curving fender and running board. my body slides sweet into the arms of age and fortune. the younger, only seven years next spring, has yet to be tested for faithfulness. already it lies about how far it has traveled. even after we fix it, we will never know the truth. some day, years from now, if it is still whole and contained, will it lie about its age? are they two horses here? after all, this is a barn. somewhere, the smell of hay. last night I saw a bicycle drive through straw and become a miracle. was it a miracle when these two beasts turned into cars?

two horses outside the barn, and me inside. graceful with age, will I saddle up some day and ride?

there is a round table here. I want to steal it. to take it home with me. a souvenir of quiet mornings. as the sun hits and grazes this roundness, I, too, feel full.

I love the closing off of the spider's nest at the top. where I can see it. the sealing off. for protection. I see now that the nest has woven itself. a woman here tends the weaving, and a man tends the woman. but the nest weaves itself, and the woman, also, lives herself. closing and sealing. for protection. that is her giving.

you see, there is a crossroads between the wood and the pole. a mesh of fence with weeds and shadows. collisions and transformations. another kind of weaving. or knot.

the barn cracks and stills, stills and cracks. in the night I waken to all the sounds. in the day I live with them and add my own. breathing deeply. a song.

during the day it is a ritual. I find special stones and grass, live weeds and bones everywhere I go. each day something new is revealed, an unraveling from the day before. at night the demons come. I get more used to them. I call them by their real names now. small artifacts protect me. I wait for the demons to lose their heat in the cooling air of morning sounds. I wait for that air and the reassurance of the day.

What makes this thing go anyway?

at the heart of the road
where the speed picks up
and it swings,
cars call to each other
like atoms
of familiar compounds

on my street live men
who hunt and gather old cars
and plant them like hope
in front of my house
I shout at them:
"who owns these cars?"

Americans name their cars and their guns
missing the matter every time:
how the metal and grease of potential
to go and go faster
is no animal, no mate

it is the attraction
of one thing to the other
speed to earth
flying objects to time
cars catching up with light
until the road swings
and my street lives on
into the next century
a survivor
of unidentifiable, unnameable
energy

Holy Planet

the window is a pregnant hope
the war, a stubborn matter
with brain around the sun
and heart transfixed at moon
life as it stands
is still left
an endless splendor
this green tree
that still blue feather

Into the Century, Next

sanctified frenzy:
what provokes
and what provides
the curing
and the killing;
the birthing
and the betting;
just know: she be the sign
but not the saint

here we sit
such tender monsters
poised
in rubble parks
poised too late?

>   will you ghost or will you angel?
>   will you break or mend?
>   how do spirits settle
>   when a planet's at its end?

how/ gentle green spot were you ever after simple? how/ circle
wet and whole did you grow a spine? which winter did you
hide in? where/ did you dissemble, that certain place divine?
life on life, and earth to earth. cracking as we go. life on life, and
earth to earth, packing as we go.

>   take your blue
>   and take your wander
>   take your slip and shelf
>   take your house
>   and take your squander
>   take your children
>   and take yourself

take the stone
and take the bone
bless your home
and give

spirits blue and spirits red
elude your fate
and live

"It happens"

an old Yiddish proverb, as in "shit happens"

the car
like a cat
quicked
across
the street
size
didn't matter
speed
was it

like a car
the cat screeched
at the light
life didn't matter
time
was hit
"you're it,"
it shouted,
and split

ALIVE

Stylus

I wanted a red pen for that one
oh, where is my red pen? permanent.
ah and ah, again.

I wanted the blue pen for love
the black ink for politics
the purple for disappearing dreams
and fantasies.

"and why," you ask
"this obsession with pens?"

"it is breath," I say
"like breathing."

"oh, poor dear,"
you sigh
"lost and dependent
on art—
devoted

"to fake beliefs
transparent wishes
dipping
diving
into ink
and lies."

"but," I whisper
"the lie curves
and makes belief
out of
this make-believe,

"and I see
what I never
saw before

"and what
I didn't know
I knew."

On Receiving Two Postcards
on the Same Day

Spring 1975

time stilled on a Saturday
of coffee and rain
moods flying low
catching cold
 but the mail is air
 and love on wings
 the mail is space of time
 and things
 the mail was sweet
 it came through twice
 picture cards from dreams and spice
Michael in Mexico
Robert in China
the poet tastes citrus/mahogany blends
 illusion's ends
 illusion's ends
the plumber sings of workers' chants
 seeds and plants
 seeds and plants
their stamps were birds
and Aztec gods
their stamps were colors
slightly spring
Michael in small hand
Robert in large calligraphy
were telling me
of my two selves
the poet and the worker
the dreamer and the thinker
they're building other worlds
out there

and I must choose, I must choose
     but the mail is air
     and love on wings
     the mail is space of time
     and things
     the mail was sweet
     it came through twice
     picture cards from dreams and spice
there are one thousand women
in my breast
I dance and dream and sing
there are hands and heads
for all the roads
songs of work
seas of soil
the work a poem
the poem a work
     the mail was sweet
     it came through twice
     picture cards from dreams and spice

Alive

in California they give you tickets for jaywalking. my grandfather got one when he moved to L.A. from Chicago at age 75. in Chicago, jaywalking is an art. if you don't cross on the red light, they think you're asleep, but the drivers have no courtesy either. during a visit back there, I got off a bus, and a motorcycle nearly killed me. it's an art, you see, staying alive.

the sweetness of craft. the timing it just right. the forever circling in. the deeper riff. jazz and melodious, musical highlight. spotlight.

my mother used to play "Summertime" all day long. like a baby cooing, it was my lullaby. the easy living. I kept hearing that song everywhere I went. then one day when I was grown and looking for a place to rent, I met this man who said he was George Gershwin. he had one of those commemorative stamps in his wallet so I could match its profile with his. he said there were a couple of vacant flats on the street, but I doubted I could afford them. I doubted I could believe him. ghosts don't talk to you about plain things like flats for rent. then he started talking about his piano and the blue bees in his head. I had to believe him. my mother's mysteries and the rhapsody everywhere I went.

conning a child to sleep with a lullaby. an old poet's crazy dream. purple palm trees. singing birds, and the bees, you see, the bees. and an unknown voice on the phone you could listen to forever. a wrong number you woke out of sleep. to be intimate with a perfect stranger.

night after night, you seem perfect, stranger. possession locks up love, and lets only disaster escape. it's unexpected delight that I'm after.

alive, that's the best part of it. it's being alive.

Song

when the song
was dug up
and placed
into the arms
of the darkest night,
it knew
it would be a bird;
after *that*
knowing
came the feather,
and *then*
the choice of flight
as maneuver
and movement.

and you
always thought
birds
came first,
that song
was a way
to copy birds
in their joy.

no, what was
was that
first
came song;
it was bird,
bird
who followed
song
into the night.

The Economy of Use

my father's father ate bone marrow
my mother's mother liked fish heads
the genes got to me
I love the cracking of bone
the sucking of marrow
friends hold noses
warn of choking
my mother asks me to take myself
and my bone from the table
the riches and knowledge I have
inherited
from very poor and very wise people
who know
everything matters

the economy of use
the wish and the dream
made live, cooked raw
devoured
growing out from my limbs
a river of red
a sea of sparkling eyes
you touch me
I hold resources
no one ever bothered to record
they threw it out
with the skin
the seeds, the veins
the tail
the head, the bone
the leaves
the brown
oh, garbage
I revere

your lucky pit
I revere what they call
waste and nuisance
the unnecessary
the uncookable
the nonfunctional
core,
lonely and rotting
from neglect
the wish and the dream
the marrow and the eye
the poetry
the stuff some say
don't matter
I say
matter
most of all